Table of Contents

Preface

Many are blessed to grow up in Norway, to know from their heart the unique foods and traditions of a Norwegian Christmas. Many more have not had that opportunity. This book and its resources are for you.

If you have dreamed of going to Norway for the Christmas season, you can become prepared to make the most of your incredible trip. If you have recently moved to Norway and wonder about all that surrounds you then you can quickly get up to speed and participate to the fullest. If you are far from Norway, we can show you the way home.

Build a heritage of home for your friends and family. Wherever you are in the world, Norway can be in your house for a season and in your heart for eternity. Make the memories yours; leave a legacy of home for those you love.

Traditions

Cast of Characters

Julenissen (Santa Claus)

Julenissen has become more like an American Santa Claus over the years, but this is not who he really is. He is not Father Christmas.

Julenissen is a man of human size who loves children. He isn't shy. He can be found in towns, schools, and shops all through December and January. He may visit children's homes on Christmas Eve. He visits to reward those who have done well and gives them chocolates, nuts, or a small gift.

Julenissen established formal residency and a workshop in Drobak, approximately 20 miles south from Oslo. This is where children receive their mail.

Reindeer

Norway's reindeer are accustomed to walking on snowy ground. Julenissenis dragged to the doors of homes by a handful of reindeer. None of them fly or dance on rooftops.

Nisser or Fjosnisser

Fjosnisser is a unique breed of gremlins that live in family barns across Norway. They are responsible for the care of crops and animals, and they expect respect in the form a warm bed and big bowls of porridge. They can live up to hundreds of years, if at all.

It is very rare to see these sneaky guys so their height is unknown. According to rumors, they are between 15 cm (6 inches) and about waist high. Nisserlooks like a garden-gnome with a pointed red hat and a large white beard. He wears a sweater with a belt, long woolen pants with knee socks, and a sweater with sleeves. His shoes are the kind of sturdy footwear required for farm work. Students may celebrate their hard work with a nissefest. Pa laven SitterNissen is a holiday song that children sing. It describes how Nisser tries to eat Christmas porridge with the mice.

He was fed up with barn rats until he got a cat to keep them away. Then he could eat in peace.

They are sensitive to slights and temperamental, possibly due to their extreme age, compensating for his stature, annoyance at pests, heavy workload or some trait in personality. He enjoys a pint or two of Christmas beer.

On Christmas Eve, families would serve a large bowl of porridge such as Risengrynsgrot or *Rommegrot*. Everything is fine if it is gone by Christmas morning. Beware if it isn't, These shrewd guys can cause as little as a spilled milk pail and barking at your dogs when you go to sleep. Or as serious as crop failure. To be safe, keep a barncat and set up a comfortable bed for Nisser in a warm, dry area.

Seasonal Calendar

Norway has a wonderful and long holiday season that brings light into the winter darkness!

Advent

While the United States uses the day following Thanksgiving to kick off Christmas, it is important to remember that the holiday does not exist elsewhere. Advent in Norway begins on December 1st, to begin the countdown to Christmas. The house is decorated with purple accents on four Sundays leading up to Christmas. Four purple candles are placed at a location of special significance. On the first Sunday, one candle is lit. The second Sunday, the first and second candles are lit. During candle lighting, there are many traditional songs and poems you can share. On the first Sunday in Advent, many community tree lighting ceremonies take place.

The Advent calendar is another tradition that can be used in many ways. One variation is to use a whole orange and push 24 cloves through thick skin. One fragrant clove is taken out each day until there are no more. A nice, hanging cloth with 24 pockets, can also be used. The pockets can hold small trinkets or little packets of nuts, chocolates or notes. A nice alternative is to buy a nicely decorated cardboard. The front has tiny, numbered doors that open to reveal a treat, similar to chocolate.

Santa Lucia Day is a day that is more popular in Italy, Denmark, and Sweden than it is in Italy. Lucia DagenDecember 13th is dedicated to the Italian Saint

Lucy, who performed many good deeds before she was martyred. The crown of battery-operated candles is worn by the crown's bearded eldest child, traditionally the oldest girl in the household. Other children may also wear white. In some places, there might be a concert or parade at the church.

Jultid **Christmas Time**

Norway's Christmas season is a wonderful time. Julenissen, reindeer and nisser are as beautiful as the Northern Lights in the mountains and fjords. Families gather to create miracles in the kitchen and enjoy cookies and legends by the fireside.

Visit your neighbors and share coffee and Julefryd (Christmas joy)
Norwegians start preparing for holidays as early as autumn. Fish is dried or smoked, sausages are stuffed and cold cuts are cured. Root vegetables such beets, onions, and garlic are pickedled for the coming celebrations.
The month leading up to Christmas is dedicated to decorating, shopping and even more cooking. In a mad rush to clean the house from top-to-bottom, spring is often left for other countries. nissefest is a party that involves children from school. They sing and dance around the Christmas tree, while Santa visits with small treats such as nuts, raisins, and oranges.
Gifts are usually practical and unpretentious, such as food, wine or decor.
Presents are purchased or made and wrapped in a simple way that demonstrates that the thought behind it is more valuable than the item inside.
Norway's holiday is a combination of anticipation and preparation. Norwegians enjoy the holiday season by preparing first and then taking a break to enjoy the 12 to 20 days of Christmas.

Little Christmas Eve: December 23rd

Although Little Christmas Eve isn't counted in the 12 days of Christmas, it is an occasion to gather with friends and kick off the season. Friends and families enjoy hot chocolate and Christmas cookies. The Christmas tree is decorated with lights and love.

Christmas Eve: December 24th

Norway's Christmas season doesn't begin until December 24th at dinnertime. All of the last-minute chores are completed during the day and work is put aside. At 4 pm, shops and offices close. Most businesses close their doors or work at a reduced hour during the first week of Christmas. The country is relaxed because everyone has planned ahead.

Many people go to church on Christmas Eve afternoon, including His Majesty.

The King of Norway. The celebrations are dominated by Lutherans and include beautiful singing and candles.

Christmas dinner is formal affair that requires a large table. A spectacular feast of meats, potatoes and vegetables is created by the use of crystal, porcelain, and good linens. The holiday season is filled with candles that burn brightly. After all that, a visitor arrives at your door. A friend or family member dress as Julenissenand arrives in person with a bag full of presents. Instead of giving a hearty ho ho, ho ho, he asks a crucial question: "Are any good children here?" Families often dance and sing around the Christmas tree. The presents from the tree are followed up by hot chocolate and coffee for the children. There is also plenty of dessert to go around - it's enough food for one.

Christmas Day: December 25th

A smorgasbord of breakfasts is served on the second day of Christmas. There are many options: boiled eggs, sweet and fruity Christmas breads, specialty cold cuts and open-face sandwiches, smoked caviar and heart-shaped waffles. Families often take advantage of the limited amount of sunlight to go on a hike, or do other outdoor activities. Then they polish off the day with delicious leftovers for dinner. Many of these are even better the next day.

Christmas Day 2: December 26th

Boxing Day is also known as Andre Juledag (Second Christmas Day) and is a day for families where the Norwegian flag can be flown and banks are shut down.

Romjul (After Christmas)

The Days Following Christmas

Romjul is the period between Christmas and New Years. These days are used to visit extended families, travel, or simply take a break from the hustle and bustle of preparations. Festive dinners continue!

Nyttar (New Year)

The Sixth Day Of Christmas: December 31st. New Year's Eve

His Majesty, King of Norway, addresses the nation on New Year's Eve. Citizens flock to the television to hear his speech. Families enjoy a large dinner together with their holiday favorites later in the evening. People dress up in formal wear to enjoy the evening across the country. Many communities light fireworks at midnight for everyone to enjoy.

The Seventh Day Of Christmas: January 1, New Year's Day

The Prime Minister gives a speech on New Year's Day that is broadcast live on television. Although it isn't as popular as King's speech on New Year's Day, people play games with him during his appearance.

The Twelfth Day Of Christmas: January 6th, Three Kings Day

January 6th is believed to have been the day that the three kings visited the Christ child in the manger (Epiphany). The day is celebrated by many churches. Many people enjoy a nice meal and wrap up the Christmas season.

Just a little more...

For the 20th day of Christmas, some celebrate until January 13. Once sparkling trees have become firewood, decorations are taken to the barn or attic, and the quiet of fat snowflakes ishes over people like the memories of past seasons and hopes for the holidays ahead.

Trimming the Tree

Norway Spruce or a real pine are the traditional Christmas tree in Norway.
Norway is home to fewer artificial trees than the United States. A live tree is
possible, but Norwegians don't celebrate Christmas for more than twenty days.
The tree should not be brought in until December 23rd.

Because carol singing and dancing around the tree are holiday traditions, it is
best to place the tree at least a few feet away from obstacles.

Traditional lighting of the tree involved small candles that were attached to the
trunk. This dangerous but beautiful practice has been abandoned in favor of
safety. Solid white lights reflect the history of candles best, while colored
lights are rarely used.

Decorations for the tree are often made from paper and usually created at home
with family members. The most popular Christmas colors are red and white.
The most traditional paper goods are the heart-shaped and cone-shaped baskets
that contain small candies, nuts, clementine oranges or chocolates. The
kremmerhus cones and julekurver hearts are both called kremmerhus .

A garland of Norwegian flags made from plain white string and Norwegian
paper is very traditional for the tree. These flags measure approximately 1 inch
in height. These flags can be bought at a Scandinavian store or online. The
appendix contains instructions and flags that you can print at home.

You can often see different styles of chains made from paper loops in grade
school. If you don't use flags, whole lengths of paper chains can be used to
create a garland for the entire tree. Or, individual ornaments can be made from

segments of paper chain with three to four loops.

Tinsel, glass balls, ribbon, wood, or shiny bead garland are all used.

Although they look more Swedish than Norwegian, there are some Norwegian Christmas trees.

Straw ornaments are great for display. They are tied with red string to appeal to our national love for all things natural and can be arranged in a variety of shapes.

When decorating your Norwegian Christmas tree, less is more. The tree should have enough space between the objects to let the natural beauty shine through. Norwegians are extremely environmentally conscious. Many Norwegian families have a woodstove or fireplace to keep them warm during winter. The ornaments are taken out of the tree and taken outside for firewood.

Recipes

Beverages

These are traditional alcoholic beverages:

Aquavit is Norway's national beverage. It stands for water of life. This bold, potato-based spirit is flavored with anise and caraway seeds, coriander, coriander, garlic, dill, and other herbs. It is a great accompaniment to Christmas food. It can be served at room temperature or cold, with no mixers.

Brennevin is a strong, very intense wine. It is very popular in Scandinavia, where it is made from potatoes or grains. You can find it in many flavors, depending on the addition of ingredients. Aquavit is a type Brennevin.

Gloggis a combination of wine or juice and spices. It tastes similar to Wassail and mulled cider.

Hard Cider is quite common. It can be served cold during the summer but is heated to combat winter chill when it comes time for Christmas. It can be spiced to taste similar to mulled grape wine.

Mead is a honey wine. It is one of the oldest beverages. It tastes almost exactly like beer. It can be made with a variety of ingredients, including fruit, spices and hops.

Øl is a popular beer in Norway. There are four types depending on the alcohol content, which can range from 0% to 7%. There are several types based on the ingredients. Juleol is a Christmas beer that's only available during the holidays.

Punch is sometimes called a Norwegian drink. However, it is more popular in Sweden and Finland. It's made from Arrack base spirit, sugar, water, fruits juices, a mix of spices and even liqueurs. It is usually served hot in winter. It is not American punch.

Non-alcoholic beverages

Coffee is everywhere. This must be why Vikings were able to row across oceans and climb mountains. It doesn't grow in our cold country!

Hot Chocolate or *Kako* is a traditional Christmas treat. It is usually made in large batches and served with a punch-like ladle. There are many hot chocolate recipes in Norway, but all of them include milk and a sweetener.

Julebrus is a fizzy red soda made especially for Christmas.

Solo is a fizzy orange soda that's loved all year.

Water may seem obvious, but Norway is careful about its environment. It has many excellent springs and wells that make it an excellent choice. Voss and Isbre Glacier Water seem to be familiar brands.

Bread

Julekake (**Christmas Bread**)

3/4 cup butter 5 cups milk

1 package yeast

7 cups all-purpose bread flour or bread flour, not for self-rising

1/2 cup sugar

1 teaspoon salt

1 cup golden raisins

3/4 cup raisins

1 1/2 cup citron (candied citrus peel)

3/4 cup chopped candied cherries, red-green mixed, cut into quarters

1 egg plus 1 teaspoon of water, lightly beat for topping

- · Mix all ingredients except the egg mix, and then knead them together.

- · Keep the dough covered in warm, draft-free water until it doubles.

- · Divide into three portions

- · Form loaves, and bake in loaf pans until doubled.

- · Spread the egg mixture on top of the loaves.

- · Bake for 20 minutes at 350°F until golden brown.

- · You can glaze the tops of the cooled bread with 3/4 cup powdered sugar and 3/4 teaspoon almond extract.

Serve cooled bread cut into slices and topped with butter.

gjetost (sweet brown goat cheese).

You can also use this dough to make a pastry. See next recipe.

Julekake **Wreath**

1 egg white, whipped until soft peaks 1 teaspoon almond extract

3/4 cup finely ground almonds 2 cups sifted sugar

Recipe *Julekake* (Christmas Bread) dough, made once

1. Make a paste by combining almond extract, almonds and beaten eggs.

2. Roll *Julekakedough* to a rectangle of approximately 1/2 inch thickness.

3. Use almond paste to cover the dough.

4. To cover the middle third of the dough, fold the long edge of the rectangle 1/3 of the length.

5. Fold the bottom 1/3 of the dough over the top and middle layers to hide the paste.

6. Divide the dough into three equal parts.

7. Each piece should be made into a circle on the cookie sheet.

8. Let the dough rest in a warm place, away from drafts, until it doubles.

9. Bake at 350°F for 15-20 minutes, or until golden brown and hollow when lightly tapped on top.

10. You can glaze the tops of the cooled bread with 3/4 cup powdered sugar and 3/4 teaspoon of rum extract. For additional decoration, sprinkle with chopped candied fruits or slivered almonds.

Slices can be served with coffee or as a snack for breakfast.

Julekake **Wreath**

Cups of warm milk 1 packet yeast

3/4 cup soft butter 7 cups flour

1/4 teaspoon sugar

1 teaspoon cardamom

1 1/2 cups raisins

For topping, beaten egg and

1 1/4 teaspoons of water

1. Let the yeast sit for 5 minutes in warm milk.

2. Combine all remaining ingredients, except egg topping, to form a smooth, shiny dough.

3. Let the dough rest in a warm place, away from drafts, until it doubles in size.

4. Divide the dough into four pieces

5. Each piece should be rolled into a sausage-like shape.

6. Each sausage shape can be cut into eight equal-sized pieces.

7. Each piece should be rolled into a ball.

8. Place the rolls on a cookie tray and let them rest until they are doubled in size.

9. Use egg mixture to brush the tops.

10. Bake for approximately 15 minutes at 325°F

Rolls

2 1/2 cup warm water

2 boxes yeast

7 cups all-purpose flour

2 tablespoons of butter

2 teaspoons salt

2 tablespoons sugar

1. Let the yeast sit for five minutes in warm water before you sprinkle it on.

2. Combine all ingredients to form a dough.

3. Let the dough rest in a warm place, away from drafts, until it doubles in size.

4. Form into two loaves or 32 rolls, and then place in baking dishes.

5. Let the dough rest until it doubles in size.

6. Bake at 325°C. Rolls should bake for approximately 15 minutes Bread takes approximately 45 minutes.

Wheat Bread

2 1/2 cups warm Water 2 boxes yeast

5 cups whole wheat flour 2 cup all-purpose flour 2 tablespoons of butter

Salt 1 teaspoon

2 tablespoons sugar

2 tablespoons vegetable oils

1. Use warm water to dissolve the sugar.

2. Let the yeast sit for five minutes in warm water before you sprinkle it on.

3. Combine all ingredients to form a dough.

4. Let the dough rest in a warm place, away from drafts, until it doubles in size.

5. Divide into two loaves and place in greased loaf pans.

6. Let the dough rest until it doubles in size.

7. Bake for 45 minutes at 325°F. Bake the bread until it is golden brown. It should sound hollow when you tap on it.

Side Dishes

Pickled Herring

4 salted herring, boned, cleaned, and cut into 1" strips

1 onion thinly sliced

8 bay leaves

¾ teaspoons whole peppercorns

½ cup apple cider vinegar

½ cup sugar

1. Rinse the herring in cold water for about 10 minutes.

2. Dry the fish well with paper towels.

3. In a wide mouth canning jar place a layer of fish about an inch deep. Cover with a few pieces of onion and some spices. Repeat until the jar is full.

4. Stir the sugar and vinegar in a small bowl until the sugar dissolves. Pour over the fish, being certain all the pieces are covered.

5. Cover the jar and marinate 3 days before eating. Do not eat the bay leaves.

6. Store in the refrigerator. Do not drain the liquid.

Pickled herring is delicious on crackers, eggs, or sandwiches.

Sour Cream Pickled Herring

2 cups pickled herring, above

4 bay leaves

1 cup Sour Cream

2 tablespoons dill leaves

1. After marinating in the vinegar solution at least 3 days, drain the fish

and pat it dry.

2. Mix dill and sour cream in a medium bowl.

3. Stir in fish to coat with sour cream.

4. Place fish in a canning jar with a bay leaf every few layers.

5. Cover the jar and store in the refrigerator.

Main Dishes

Potato Sausage

8 pounds raw shredded potatoes

2 pounds raw hamburger meat

3 pounds raw ground pork

3 medium raw onions, finely chopped

3 tablespoons salt

1 teaspoon pepper

1 teaspoon allspice

Sausage skins

1. Shred potatoes into water to retain the pale color. A food processor makes quick work of this step.

2. Mix all other ingredients together, except the sausage skins.

3. Drain the potatoes, pat them dry, and add them to the mixture.

4. Stuff mixture into the sausage skins, creating a full sausage with no empty gaps, but not so full that they burst when cooked.

   · Tie off the ends using basic kitchen twine. Sausages may be made into hot dog lengths, or a big loop about 18 inches long.

   · If you don't have sausage skins, shape the meat into a long roll about an inch in diameter. Wrap the meat firmly in 3 layers of plastic wrap. Poke the plastic wrap about six times along the length so they don't rupture when cooked.

5. Refrigerate the sausages for 2 days, to let the flavors marry.

6. Cook the sausages in lightly boiling water for 15 to 20 minutes, depending on thickness.

7. If longer term storage is desired, the sausages may be frozen or salted in brine.

8. The sausages may be served with gravy (below), or mustard. Boiled potatoes are always a good side dish. Ketchup or a bun is not traditional.

Spiced White Gravy

¾ cup butter

2 ½ tablespoons all-purpose flour

2 teaspoons sugar

3 cup milk

½ teaspoon ground nutmeg

1. Melt butter in a frying pan over medium high heat.

2. Add all-purpose flour and stir briskly to combine into a paste.

3. Stirring constantly add milk and cook for a few minutes to remove the raw flavor from the flour.

4. Do not allow the ingredients to brown; remove from the heat to stop the browning.

5. Add sugar and nutmeg.

Meatballs and Gravy

Meatballs

2 pounds ground beef

1 egg

1 tablespoon all-purpose flour

½ cup of fresh minced onions

2 cloves minced garlic

1 teaspoon salt

¼ teaspoon ground black pepper

1. Mix all the ingredients until they stick together. The easiest way is to dampen your clean hands and knead. A dough hook on a large stand mixer would also work.

2. Shape the meatballs by putting a heaping tablespoon of meat into the palm of your hands and rolling it into a ball with the other hand.

3. Fry the meatballs over medium high heat, turning occasionally until evenly browned and cooked medium well.

4. Remove from heat and make the following gravy. If desired, meatballs may be frozen before making the gravy.

Brown Gravy

1 cup of butter

¾ cup of all-purpose flour

4 cups beef broth

Salt and pepper to taste

6. Melt butter in a frying pan over medium high heat.

7. Add all-purpose flour and stir briskly to combine into a paste.

8. Stirring constantly, allow the ingredients to brown. Be aware this may take a little while and then occur suddenly. You are looking for a deep caramel color for the richest flavor, but be careful not to burn it.

9. Quickly add the broth when the color is right. Stir briskly to combine smoothly and promptly remove from the heat to stop the browning.

10. Add salt and pepper to taste. The amounts will vary depending on your broth.

To complete the dish add the hot meatballs into the gravy. Serve with boiled potatoes, carrots, and cabbage.

Chicken Fricassee

While this isn't just a Christmas recipe, we did eat this in Norway. Because we typically had a lot of fish, it was special to us. Since there were so many days in the holiday season it was an option for a lovely meal.

Braised Chicken

1 whole chicken, cut into standard pieces, with the skin on

1 teaspoon salt

½ cup chopped onions

Water, enough to cover the chicken

1. In a large pot bring the water to a boil with the salt.

2. Add the onions and chicken pieces.

3. Reduce to a simmer and stir occasionally until the chicken is fully cooked.

4. Take the chicken out of the broth and set it aside. Remove the chicken skin and bones, keeping the meat in chunks as large as possible.

5. Skim the fat off the top of the broth, saving ½ cup for the sauce.

6. Strain the broth into a storage container. Make the sauce below with some of it and save the remainder for soup or other recipes.

Sauce

½ cup of chicken fat from the braised chicken

3¼ tablespoons of all-purpose flour

1 tablespoon of mild curry, to taste

4¼ cup of chicken broth

¼ cup of minced parsley

1. In a large deep skillet heat chicken fat to boiling. Reduce heat to medium.

2. Add all-purpose flour and curry, stirring briskly to combine into a paste.

3. Stir for about a minute to remove the raw flavor from the all-purpose flour. Do not brown the mix.

4. Add the chicken broth to make a somewhat thin gravy, using more or less as needed.

5. Add the lumps of skinless chicken and simmer in the sauce for about 10 minutes. Stir occasionally so the food doesn't stick to the pan.

6. Just before serving add the parsley so it stays fresh and doesn't wilt.

Great with boiled potatoes, and carrots or parsnips.

Fårikål (Lamb and Cabbage Stew)

This is the undisputed national dish of Norway. It even has its own holiday on the last Thursday of September.

3 ½ pounds of lamb or mutton, preferably bone-in, fat untrimmed, cut into 2-3 inch chunks

1 medium cabbage, cut into 3 inch chunks

¾ cup all-purpose flour

1 teaspoon salt

¾ teaspoon whole black pepper

Cool water, to cover the ingredients

1. Arrange ⅓ of the meat on the bottom of a large pot, fat side down. Layer ⅓ of the cabbage, flour and spices over it.

2. Make three layers of these ingredients.

3. Cover the ingredients with cool water. Hot water is not recommended.

4. Simmer about 2 hours until very tender.

5. Eat while warm, or better yet, let it season in the refrigerator for a day and reheat.

Serve with boiled potatoes. It's up to you if you want to eat the whole peppers, or not. It's considered brave if you do.

Alternate Version: *Jegerkål*

Sometimes in the winter this is made as *Jegerkål* by adding 1 teaspoon each of caraway seeds and juniper berries along with the pepper corns.

Fresh Pork Roast

Fresh pork picnic shoulder, ⅓ to ½ pound of meat per person, fat covering intact

Salt

Water

1. Rinse pork and pat dry before placing in roasting pan.

2. Sprinkle with salt

3. Cover the bottom of the pan with about ¼ inch of water

4. Cover the roasting pan leaving the lid slightly ajar, or tent loosely with foil

5. Bake at 350° until internal meat temperature reaches 145 °

6. Remove from oven.

7. Cut the heavy fat covering off of the roast and place it on a cookie sheet or jelly roll pan with an edge.

8. Tent the meat with foil to keep it warm and let the juices draw back into the meat.

9. Cut diamond shapes about halfway into the fat using diagonal lines (#) about an inch apart.

10. Bake the fat at 350° for 8-10 minutes until toasty tan color, being careful not to burn it.

11. Serve the crispy fat with the meat.

Serve with boiled potatoes and _Sur Kål_. A brown gravy may be made from the leftover broth.

Desert

Caramel Pudding

Custard

2½ cups milk

1⅔ cups cream

4 eggs

4 tablespoons sugar

1 teaspoon vanilla sugar

1. Stirring frequently, cook ingredients in a medium saucepan over medium heat until the sugars dissolve. Do not boil.

2. Remove from heat and cool to room temperature.

3. Make the caramel sauce below.

Caramel Sauce

2 cups sugar

1 cup water

1. Shake sugar in a frying pan over medium heat until it begins to melt and turn brown. Do not stir.

2. Add the water and shake the pan occasionally until the sugar has fully dissolved and the sauce is brown.

Caramel Pudding

1. Place six ramekins in a 9 x 13 inch rectangular cake pan.

2. Put 1 tablespoon of the caramel sauce in the bottom of each ramekin then fill with cooled custard.

3. Create a water bath for the pudding by adding water to the cake pan to

match the level of custard in the individual cups.

4. Bake at 250° for about an hour, or until a knife inserted in the center of the custard comes out clean.

5. Let cool until the cups can be safely handled.

6. Run a knife around the edge of each cup to loosen the pudding.

7. Place a small desert dish firmly over the ramekin and quickly flip it to invert the pudding and keep the caramel sauce.

This is a similar to flan. Serve with a dollop of whipped cream, if desired, and strong Norwegian coffee.

Risengrynsgrøt (Rice Pudding)

1 cup of pearl rice, or other small grain rice

1½ cup water

½ teaspoon salt

1 cup whole milk

½ pint of whipping cream, whipped with 1 teaspoon of vanilla and ½ cup of sugar

¾ cup of chopped unsalted almonds, raw is preferred, roasted is okay

1 whole almond, peeled

1. In a medium saucepan bring rice to a boil with the water, salt, and milk.

2. Reduce to a simmer and cook until the rice is tender, stirring occasionally.

3. Chill rice mixture in the refrigerator until fully cold.

4. Fold the whipped cream and nuts into the rice.

5. Top with strawberry sauce and sweetened cream, below.

Strawberry Sauce

4 cups of cleaned and topped strawberries, cut into quarters

2 cups water

¼ cup sugar

2 tablespoons corn starch mixed with ½ cup cold water until smooth

1. In a medium saucepan stir all ingredients.

2. Cook over a medium heat, stirring frequently, until the sauce is transparent.

3. Chill the sauce in the refrigerator.

Place the rice pudding in individual bowls. If the one whole almond shows, tuck it into the pudding and smooth it over so it is hidden. Top with strawberry sauce.

It is traditional for the person who finds the whole almond in their pudding to win a small prize, usually a marzipan pig.

Sviskegrøt (**Prune Pudding**)

1½ pounds soft dried prunes, pitted

6 cups cold water, ¼ cup reserved

¾ cup sugar, plus 2 tablespoons reserved

4 tablespoons potato starch, may substitute corn starch

1 cup of whipped cream sweetened with 1 teaspoon of vanilla and ½ cup of sugar

1. Over medium heat stew prunes in water and sugar until tender.
2. Stir starch in ¼ cup of cold water until dissolved, add to hot mixture and stir.
3. When starch has become clear in the pudding remove from heat.
4. Put pudding into a serving bowl or several individual bowls.
5. Sprinkle reserved sugar lightly over the top of the pudding.
6. Chill in the refrigerator until cold.

Serve chilled prune pudding topped with whipped cream or sweetened cream.

Sweetened Cream

¾ cup of half and half

2 tablespoons of sugar

1. In a small bowl lightly stir ingredients until sugar dissolves.
2. The cream should remain liquid. The goal is not whipped cream.

Cookies

Pepperkaker (Pepper Cookies)

1 egg

¾ cup brown sugar

¼ teaspoon salt

¾ cup shortening

¾ cup molasses

1 teaspoon ginger

1 teaspoon cinnamon

¼ teaspoon ground pepper

¼ teaspoon cloves

2 cups sifted all-purpose flour

1. Mix all ingredients, except flour

2. Add flour and mix thoroughly

3. Place dough in a cookie press with the disk that looks like a crown, a long thin line that is flat on the bottom and jagged on the top.

4. Press the cookie dough in parallel strips that go from one end of a lightly greased cookie sheet to the other the long way, stopping about an inch from the end. When you have created enough strips to fill the cookie sheet, release the pressure on the press and set it aside.

   · If you do not have a cookie press, the dough can be rolled into a 3 inch log, put in plastic wrap, refrigerated, and cut into ¼ inch slices.

   · If you want to decorate your tree, roll the dough ¼ inch thick and cut into heart, tree, or pig shapes. Put a hole in the top center of the cookie to thread a string through.

5. Carefully cut your strips of cookie dough into segments about 3½ inches long. They should lay flat on the cookie sheet. If they pull up with you cutting tool, then gently lay them back down taking care not to disturb the ridged pattern.

6. Bake at 350° for 6-8 minutes until just barely browned at the edges.

Spritz Cookies

¾ cup sugar

1 cup butter, room temperature

1 teaspoon vanilla

¼ teaspoon salt

2¼ cup all-purpose flour

1 egg yolk

1 egg white, lightly beaten

Sugar sprinkles

1. Cream sugar and butter until fluffy.

2. Beat in vanilla, salt, flour, and egg yolk.

3. Place dough in cookie press.

4. Use the disk of your choice like star, tree, or wreath.

   · If you do not have a cookie sheet the dough can be rolled ¼ inch thick and cut with cookie cutters.

5. Create shapes about an inch apart on lightly greased cookie sheet.

6. Brush cookies with beaten egg white and sprinkle with sugar sprinkles.

7. Bake at 350° for 8-10 minutes, cookies should be fairly light in color.

Sandbakkels

1 cup butter, room temperature

2 eggs

2 ¾ cups sifted all-purpose flour

1 teaspoon almond extract

1 cup sugar

1. Mix all the ingredients until they stick together.

2. Take about a teaspoon of dough and press it evenly to the sides and bottom of sandbakkel tins.

3. Bake at 350° for 8-10 minutes.

4. Gently and immediately remove the cookies from the tins. They will stick if they cool off, so they can be slightly reheated if you can't get them out.

These are crisp, tasty cookies that are lovely to serve as-is. They may also be filled like little tarts with glazed fruit, custard, or other ingredients.

Krumkake

2 ½ cups sugar

1 ½ cups butter

3 eggs

1¼ cup flour

½ teaspoon cardamom

1. Mix all the ingredients to create a thin batter.

2. Determine what shape you want for your cookies and prepare your tools.

    · A cone shape is traditional, but a bowl shape or tube is also useful.

    · If you are new to these cookies they can also be laid flat to cool, but shapes are much more elegant and traditional.

3. Heat your _krumkake_ iron to the temperature suggested by the manufacturer.

4. Place one tablespoon of dough in the center of the bottom plate of the open iron, then close the top.

5. Bake each cookie approximately a minute per side.

    · If you have an iron that goes over a burner you will need to flip the iron over after 1 minute so the other side can cook. Keep the handles tightly closed while turning so the delicate pattern stays crisp.

    · If you have an electric _krumkake_ iron confirm with the manual that both sides will cook at the same time.

6. When lightly tan in color, quickly wrap the hot cookie around the

cone or other shape to cool.

7. Keep in an air-tight storage container to protect from humidity and keep them crisp.

Krumkake may be filled with sweetened whipped cream, whipped cream mixed with a tablespoon of jam, or other light mild filling. A bold filling will overtake the delicate flavor of the *krumkake*.

Torre Vafler **(Dry Waffle Cookies)**

4 eggs, separated

3 teaspoon baking powder

1⅓ tablespoon melted butter

1 ½ cup sugar

½ teaspoon corn starch

1 ¼ teaspoon vanilla

1. Mix all ingredients, except egg whites.

2. Beat egg whites until fluffy and gently fold into other ingredients.

3. Bake in a Scandinavian heart-shaped waffle maker until lightly browned.

4. After removing from the waffle maker, cut out each heart, and any spilled dough that goes past the designed edges.

5. Let cookies cool.

6. Store in an air-tight container.

These are considered cookies, rather than waffles. They are not topped with syrup or jam.

Walnut Crescents

1 cup soft butter

¾ cup sifted powder sugar

⅛ teaspoon salt

1 ½ teaspoon almond extract

1 cup ground walnuts, no shells

½ cup sugar

1. Mix dough and allow it to rest at room temperature for 30 minutes.

2. Roll the dough into a ½ inch thick rope.

3. Cut the rope into segments 2 ½ inches long

4. Bend the pieces into a crescent shape, pinching in the ends a little so it looks like a young moon.

5. Bake on a lightly greased cookie sheet for 8-10 minutes at 350°. Cookies should be fairly pale.

6. Cool on a wire rack then roll in powdered sugar.

7. Store in an air-tight container to protect from humidity.

8. Roll in powder sugar again before serving, if desired.

Candy

False Marzipan

¾ cup water

3½ tablespoons unsalted butter

⅔ cup flour

2.2 pounds almonds, blanched and ground to the size of flour

6 cups powdered sugar, sifted

1 teaspoon almond extract

1. Melt butter in a large sauce pan with the water.
2. Remove from heat.
3. Add remaining ingredients, beating vigorously to avoid lumps.
4. Knead the dough until it becomes a smooth ball.

Refrigerate in an airtight container. This is great for candy and in other deserts. It can be shaped, rolled, and molded. It can be used to wrap dried fruits, dipped in chocolate, or used instead of frosting over a cake. Be creative!

Knekk

1 cup sugar

1 cup golden treacle syrup

1 cup heavy cream

½ cup chopped nuts

1. In a wide heavy sauce pan simmer sugar, syrup, and cream to soft ball stage, at least 30 minutes.

   · If you can't get golden syrup where you live, use 2/3 corn syrup and 1/3 molasses for a different flavor.

2. Stir in nuts. For another variation, use shredded coconut.

3. Pour into foil candy cups.

4. Cool before eating.

Hazelnut Balls

3 ½ ounces whole hazelnuts, shelled (about 21 nuts)

¾ teaspoon instant coffee powder

5 ½ ounces milk chocolate

1. Carefully melt chocolate.

2. Stir coffee powder in warm chocolate until dissolved.

3. Stir in nuts.

4. With a teaspoon scoop up 3 nuts and the surrounding chocolate and place in a candy cup, or on waxed paper, to cool.

Norsk Burnt Almond

⅔ cup water

6 cups powdered sugar, sifted

7 ounces whole almonds

1. Stir together ingredients in saucepan over medium heat.

2. When the ingredients become dry then spread out to cool on a lightly greased cookie sheet.

Store candies in an airtight container. May be served as alone or included as an ingredient in other deserts. Nice dipped in chocolate and rolled in chopped nuts or coconut.

Lefse

Lefse is served as a snack with coffee when guests come to visit, or with other treats during the desert course.

To serve *lefse* smear the top with a paste made of butter, cinnamon, and sugar to taste. Fold the *lefse* so the butter side does not show. There are various ways to cut the *lefse*; you can choose a different style for each type of *lefse* that you are serving.

- Traditional: Fold the top and bottom quarter of the *lefse* in toward the center. Fold in half so all the butter is inside. Cut into triangles or narrow rectangles by cutting from one straight edge to the other. Feed the rounded trimming on each edge to your kitchen helpers.

- Pretty Modern Spirals: Starting on the edge, tightly roll the *lefse* into a log. Perpendicular to the edge, cut the *lefse* into pieces about an inch and a half long. Feed the rounded trimming on each edge to your kitchen helpers. Stand them on the cut edge so the spiral pattern shows on your serving plate.

- Fast Family Shortcut: Place a second *lefse* on top of the butter mixture and cut into wedges like pizza. Alternative: Starting on the edge, tightly roll the *lefse* into a log.

Tools for *Lefse*

Here are a few of the things you will want to collect for your *lefse* making kit:

- Plain or patterned rolling pin

- *Lefse* turner

- *Lefse* griddle

- Rolling cone

- Potato ricer, for potato *lefse*

Nordlandslefse (**North Country** *Lefse*)

1 quart buttermilk

1 cup butter

1 ½ cups sugar

1 egg

2 teaspoons baking powder

2 teaspoons baking soda

1 teaspoon cardamom

6 cups all-purpose flour

1. Mix ingredients together adding enough flour to make a pliable dough. Do not over mix; you are looking for a tender dough.

2. Divide the dough into balls about the size of an apple.

3. Roll out dough to circles the size of a dinner plate, about ¼ inch thick. An ordinary rolling pin is fine; however there are special patterned *lefse* rolling pins for a light, decorative, and more traditional *lefse*. Dust your rolling pin and countertop with flour if your dough is sticking.

4. Bake on an electric or stovetop griddle for about 5 minutes per side until lightly toasted.

   · As a last resort, they can also be baked on a cookie sheet in a 450° oven. You will need to watch them closely for color and may need to flip them over halfway through the baking to keep the color even on both sides.

   · A *Lefse* Turning Stick is a long narrow paddle used to flip or roll *lefse*. You will find it a welcome addition to your *lefse* making kit. In a pinch, an alternative would be a pizza paddle or long fish spatula.

5. Refrigerate the *lefse* in an airtight container if you will eat them within a couple days. Freeze for longer storage.

See serving instructions at the beginning of the *lefse* section.

Røsnes Lefse

2 cups buttermilk

9 ounces butter, room temperature

1¼ cup sugar

3 tablespoons dark corn syrup

2 ½ teaspoons baking soda

6 cups all-purpose flour

1. Mix ingredients together adding enough flour to make a pliable dough. Do not over mix; you are looking for a tender dough.

2. Divide the dough into balls the size of an apple.

3. Roll out dough to circles the size of a dinner plate, about ¼ inch thick. An ordinary rolling pin is fine; however there are special patterned *lefse* rolling pins for a light, decorative, and more traditional *lefse*. Dust your rolling pin and countertop with flour if your dough is sticking.

4. Bake on an electric or stovetop griddle for about 5 minutes per side until lightly toasted.

   · As a last resort, they can also be baked on a cookie sheet in a 450° oven. You will need to watch them closely for color and may need to flip them over halfway through the baking to keep the color even on both sides.

   · A *Lefse* Turning Stick is a long narrow paddle used to flip or roll *lefse*. You will find it a welcome addition to your *lefse* making kit. In a pinch, an alternative would be a pizza paddle or long fish spatula.

5. Refrigerate the *lefse* in an airtight container if you will eat them within a couple days. Freeze for longer storage.

See serving instructions at the beginning of the *lefse* section.

Hardanger Lefse

1 cup dark corn syrup

½ cup sugar

2 cups buttermilk

2 cups sour cream

3 teaspoons baking soda

6 cups flour

1. Heat syrup and sugar to dissolve.

2. Remove from heat.

3. Mix in buttermilk, sour cream, and baking soda.

4. Add flour to make a light, tender dough that holds together.

5. Divide the dough into balls about the size of an apple.

6. Roll out dough to circles the size of a dinner plate, about ¼ inch thick. An ordinary rolling pin is fine; however there are special patterned *lefse* rolling pins for a light, decorative, and more traditional *lefse*. Dust your rolling pin and countertop with flour if your dough is sticking.

7. Bake on an electric or stovetop griddle for about 5 minutes per side until lightly toasted.

   a. As a last resort, they can also be baked on a cookie sheet in a 450° oven. You will need to watch them closely for color and may need to flip them over halfway through the baking to keep the color even on both sides.

   b. A *Lefse* Turning Stick is a long narrow paddle used to flip or roll *lefse*. You will find it a welcome addition to your *lefse* making kit. In a pinch, an alternative would be a pizza paddle or long fish spatula.

8. Refrigerate the *lefse* in an airtight container if you will eat them within a couple days. Freeze for longer storage.

See serving instructions at the beginning of the *lefse* section.

Potetlefse (**Potato** *Lefse*)

3 pounds of Russet potatoes

2 tablespoons butter, room temperature

2 tablespoons sour cream

¼ teaspoon salt

1½ cup flour

1. Peel potatoes and boil until very tender, but not mushy. Drain well.

2. Press cooked potatoes through a potato ricer. If you don't have a ricer you can grate them.

3. Mix all ingredients and knead so the dough holds together. If it is too soft, you can add a little more flour.

4. Divide the dough into pieces about the size of a softball.

5. Roll out dough to 8" circles, about ⅓ inch thick. An ordinary rolling pin is fine; however there are special patterned *lefse* rolling pins for a light, decorative, and more traditional *lefse*. Dust your rolling pin and countertop with flour if your dough is sticking.

6. Bake on an electric or stovetop griddle for about 5 minutes per side until lightly toasted.

   a. As a last resort, they can also be baked on a cookie sheet in a 450° oven. You will need to watch them closely for color and may need to flip them over halfway through the baking to keep the color even on both sides.

   b. A *Lefse* Turning Stick is a long narrow paddle used to flip or roll *lefse*. You will find it a welcome addition to your *lefse* making kit. In a pinch, an alternative would be a pizza paddle or long fish spatula.

7. Refrigerate the *lefse* in an airtight container if you will eat them within a couple days. Freeze for longer storage.

See serving instructions at the beginning of the *lefse* section.

Index

Sour Cream Pickled Herring

Main Dishes

Potato Sausage

Meatballs and Gravy

Chicken Fricassee

Fårikål (Lamb and Cabbage Stew)

Fresh Pork Roast

Desert

Caramel Pudding

Risengrynsgrøt (Rice Pudding)

Sviskegrøt (Prune Pudding)

Cookies

Pepperkaker (Pepper Cookies)

Spritz Cookies

Sandbakkels

Krumkake

Torre Vafler (Dry Waffle Cookies)

Walnut Crescents

Candy

False Marzipan

Knekk

Hazelnut Balls

Norsk Burnt Almond

Lefse

Nordlandslefse (North Country *Lefse*)

Røsnes Lefse

Hardanger Lefse

Potetlefse (Potato *Lefse*)

Appendices

Appendix A: Norwegian Flag Tree Garland

In Norway the tree is often trimmed with small Norwegian paper flags which hang from a garland of simple string. If you would like to recreate this for the tree in your home or office instructions are available below. Because the paper could get wet outside, this project is best for indoor trees.

CAUTION: Be advised that paper is flammable so take all precautions to avoid combustion. While beautiful and traditional, burning candles are not recommended on the tree.

Items

Gather the following items:

- Simple thin white cotton string. The length needed will vary depending on the size of your tree and how close together the rows of garland are from one another - enough to wrap around your tree several times.

- Several sheets of white printer paper, matte is traditional, glossy would reflect the tree lights

- Printer with color ink

- Scissors or paper trimmer

- Double sided tape or glue suitable for paper

- Ruler or measuring tape

Instructions

1. Cut one piece of string long enough to decorate your tree.

   o Measure the height of the tree in inches and multiply that by three to find how many inches your string should be.

   o You can be certain of the correct string length by trying the plain string on the tree before attaching the flags; you don't want the flags to become accidentally damaged.

o If your string is too short you can just tie a matching piece of string to it. The knot can be hidden behind a branch or ornament.

2. Measure the length of your finished string in feet to determine how many flags you will need.

   o A quick way to do this is to measure one foot, then fold the string into matching one foot lengths and count the segments.

3. You will need three or four flags for each foot of string. Print as many copies of the flags on the following page as necessary to create enough decorations for your tree.

   o The size of the flags may be adjusted to meet the needs of your tree. A large tree can handle larger flags and, of course, a small tree can use smaller flags.

   o To adjust the size of the flags print the page at a percentage of the normal size using that feature of your printer. If you need help with this, review the owner's manual for the printer or contact the manufacturer.

4. Fold each sheet of paper down the center between the two mirrored flags.

5. Cut out each double flag.

   o To avoid misalignments of the final flag, keep the paper folded while cutting.

   o The only white should be within the flag; there should not be a white border around the outside edge.

   o Do not cut down the folded center between the two flags.

6. Attach the flags to the string by laying the string on the inside of the folded flag, along the fold line, using paper glue or double sided tape. There should be about 3 inches of bare string between flags.

   o The spacing of the flags along the string is a matter of personal taste and proportion to the tree. Smaller flags on a smaller tree should be closer together, for example.

o The adhesive should touch the string so the flag does not slide from its assigned space.

o The adhesive should touch the corners of the flag so the white paper inside of the flag does not show.

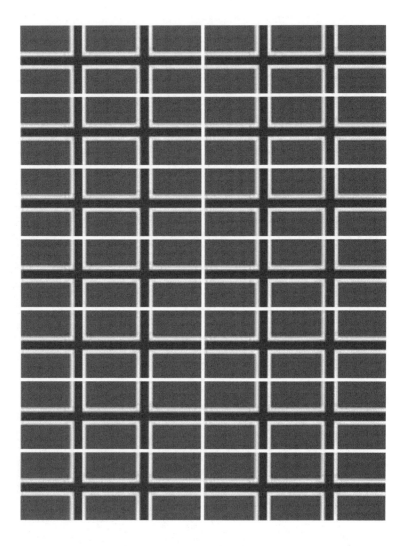

Appendix B: Online Resources

This is in no way intended to be a comprehensive list, rather a jumping off point to get you started.

Pintrest page for this book:
http://pinterest.com/justinbookcase/heritage-of-home-norwegian-christmas/

Scandinavian Shopping: Music, Decorations, Books, and more.
http://astore.amazon.com/justinllc.nc-20

Norwegian Culture Organizations

Daughters of Norway: http://www.daughtersofnorway.org/
Promoting Norwegian heritage through the sisterhood of Norwegian-Americans.

Sons of Norway: http://www.sofn.com
To promote Norwegian traditions and fraternal fellowship activities including language camps, classes, scholarships, handicrafts, cooking and heritage classes, heritage programs, sports programs, travel, *Viking Magazine*, and outreach programs sponsored by the Sons of Norway Foundation.

Norwegian Museums in the United States

Nordic Heritage Museum: http://www.nordicmuseum.org
3014 NW 67th St, Seattle, WA 98117
1-206-789-5707

Scandinavian East Coast Museum: http://www.scandinavian-museum.org
c/o LES
440 Ovington Ave, Brooklyn, NY 11209
1-718-748-5950

Vesterheim Norwegian-American Museum: http://vesterheim.org
P.O. Box 379 or 502 W. Water St
Decorah, Iowa 52101
1-563-382-9681

Genealogy

If you are interested in tracing your Norwegian heritage, it is wise to learn about family naming practices and farm names before beginning. Here are a few of many resources to get you on the right track.

Cyndi's List: http://cyndislist.com/norway
Lists of resources for researching your ancestors in Norway

Norway-Heritage: http://www.norwayheritage.com
Passenger list and emigrant ship records from Norway

Norwegian American Genealogical Center & Naeseth Library:
http://www.nagcnl.org

Roots Web: http://www.rootsweb.ancestry.com/~wgnorway/

Made in the USA
Las Vegas, NV
21 November 2021

34948535R00046